U.S. HISTORY IN REVIEW

THE CIVIL RIGHTS MOVEMENT

SETH LYNCH

Enslow PUBLISHING

Please visit our website, www.enslow.com. For a free color catalog of all our high-quality books, call toll free 1-800-398-2504 or fax 1-877-980-4454.

Library of Congress Cataloging-in-Publication Data

Names: Lynch, Seth author
Title: The civil rights movement / Seth Lynch.
Description: Buffalo, NY : Enslow Publishing, 2027. | Series: U.S. history in review | Includes index.
Identifiers: LCCN 2025025458 (print) | LCCN 2025025459 (ebook) | ISBN 9781978547056 (library binding) | ISBN 9781978547049 (paperback) | ISBN 9781978547063 (ebook)
Subjects: LCSH: African Americans–Civil rights–History–Juvenile literature | Civil rights movements–United States–Juvenile literature
Classification: LCC E185.61 .L96 2027 (print) | LCC E185.61 (ebook) | DDC 323.1196/073–dc23/eng/20250731
LC record available at https://lccn.loc.gov/2025025458
LC ebook record available at https://lccn.loc.gov/2025025459

Published in 2027 by
Enslow Publishing
2544 Clinton Street
Buffalo, NY 14224

Portions of this work were originally authored by John O'Mara and published as *The Civil Rights Movement*. All new material in this edition is authored by Seth Lynch.

Series design: Leslie Taylor
Interior layout: Tanya Dellaccio Keeney
Editor: Therese Shea

Photo credits: Series art (grunge flag) Andrey Kuzmin/Shutterstock.com; series art (stamp icon) Stocker_team/Shutterstock.com; series art (font) santstock/Shutterstock.com; series art (swash) BUTENKOV ALEKSEI/Shutterstock.com; cover (main), p. 7 (top), 9, 11, 13 (top) Courtesy of the Library of Congress; p. 5 https://upload.wikimedia.org/wikipedia/commons/4/4c/Civil_Rights_March_on_Washington%2C_D.C._%28Leaders_marching_from_the_Washington_Monument_to_the_Lincoln_Memorial%29_-_NARA_-_542010.jpg; p. 7 (bottom) https://upload.wikimedia.org/wikipedia/commons/b/b2/PollTaxRecieptJefferson1917.JPG; p. 13 (bottom) mark reinstein/Shutterstock.com; p. 15 (top) https://upload.wikimedia.org/wikipedia/commons/e/ea/Rosa_Parks_being_fingerprinted_by_Deputy_Sheriff_D.H._Lackey_after_being_arrested_on_February_22%2C_1956%2C_during_the_Montgomery_bus_boycott.jpg; p. 15 (bottom) Courtesy of the National Archives; p. 17 Pics6232/Shutterstock.com; p. 19 (top) https://upload.wikimedia.org/wikipedia/commons/5/5f/Civil_Rights_protesters_and_Woolworth%27s_Sit-In%2C_Durham%2C_NC%2C_10_February_1960._From_the_N%26O_Negative_Collection%2C_State_Archives_of_North_Carolina%2C_Raleigh%2C_NC._Photos_taken_by_The_News_%26_%2824495308926%29.jpg; p. 19 (bottom) Courtesy of U.S. Embassy The Hague/Flickr.com; p. 21 (top) https://upload.wikimedia.org/wikipedia/commons/9/9c/Exhibit_on_Freedom_Riders_-_Center_for_Civil_and_Human_Rights_-_Atlanta_-_Georgia_-_USA_%2833468216774%29.jpg; p. 21 (bottom) https://upload.wikimedia.org/wikipedia/commons/1/14/Greyhound_Bus_Attack_Anniston_1.jpg; p. 23 (top) https://upload.wikimedia.org/wikipedia/commons/8/8b/Martin_Luther_King_Jr_National_Historic_Site_%2836233249121%29.jpg; p. 23 (bottom) https://upload.wikimedia.org/wikipedia/commons/6/67/Civil_rights_march_on_Washington%2C_D.C._from_Lincoln_%28cropped%29.jpg; p. 25 https://upload.wikimedia.org/wikipedia/commons/a/a9/Lyndon_Johnson_signing_Civil_Rights_Act%2C_July_2%2C_1964.jpg; p. 27 (top) https://upload.wikimedia.org/wikipedia/commons/2/21/Malcolm_X_1963_press_photo.jpg; p. 27 (bottom) https://upload.wikimedia.org/wikipedia/commons/1/13/Malcolm_X_in_discussion.jpg; p. 29 Eli Wilson/Shutterstock.com.

Printed in the United States of America

CPSIA compliance information: Batch #CSENS27: For further information, contact Enslow Publishing, New York, New York, at 1-800-398-2504.

Contents

Fight for Rights 4
Discrimination 6
Jim Crow Laws 10
Brown v. Board 12
Brave Rosa Parks 14
Protesting Segregation 18
Marching on Washington 22
Laws for Equality 24
Malcolm X 26
King Is Killed 28
Timeline of the Civil Rights Movement 30
Glossary 31
For More Information 32
Index 32

*Words in the glossary appear in **bold** the first time they are used in the text.*

Fight for Rights

Black people were **enslaved** in parts of the United States until the end of the American Civil War (1861–1865). They became U.S. **citizens** with the Fourteenth **Amendment**. But their civil rights weren't respected. They fought for these rights during the 1950s and 1960s. This was the civil rights movement.

Learn More

Civil rights are rights, or freedoms, that belong to a country's citizens. They include the right to vote, schooling, jobs, housing, government services, and more.

Discrimination

By the 1870s, some states had passed laws that made people take tests or pay money called a poll tax to vote. This kept many Black Americans from their right to vote. They often didn't have the schooling or money that white people had.

poll tax poster

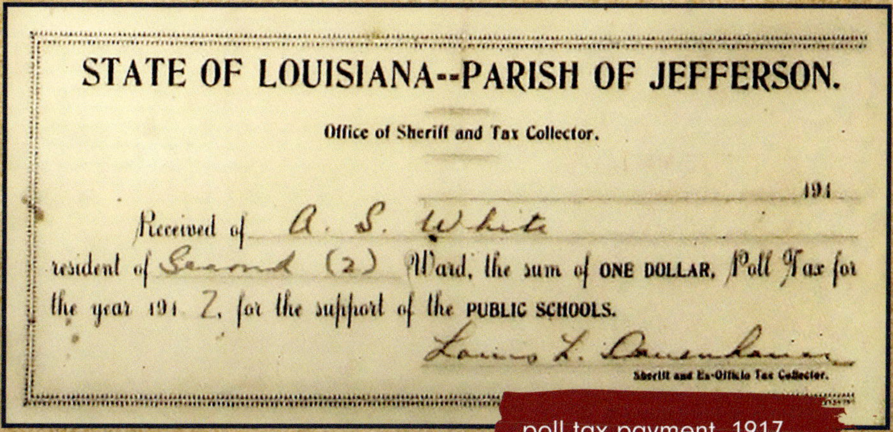

poll tax payment, 1917

Learn More

Some state laws only allowed people to vote if their grandfather had. So, Black Americans whose grandfathers were enslaved couldn't vote.

Black Americans faced discrimination in many places in the United States. In 1896, the high court in the United States, the U.S. Supreme Court, ruled that "separate but equal" public **facilities** were lawful. This allowed segregation, or the separation of **races**. And often, the facilities weren't equal.

Learn More

Discrimination is unfairly treating people unequally because of race, beliefs, or another feature.

Jim Crow Laws

More than half of all U.S. states had laws that kept Black and white Americans separate. These laws were called Jim Crow laws. They allowed separate schools, restaurants, shops, and parks. There were even separate **cemeteries**. Jim Crow laws were found throughout the South.

Learn More

Signs in states with Jim Crow laws sometimes used the word "colored." Today, this term is **offensive**.

Brown v. Board

A group called the NAACP (National Association for the Advancement of Colored People) fought for equality using the courts. A case called *Brown v. Board of Education of Topeka* reached the Supreme Court. In 1954, the court ruled that "separate but equal" schools were unconstitutional.

integrated classroom

Learn More

Unconstitutional means going against the U.S. Constitution. A constitution lists the basic laws of a country.

Brave Rosa Parks

Even after *Brown v. Board*, segregation continued. In 1955, a Black woman in Montgomery, Alabama, named Rosa Parks refused to give her bus seat to a white man. She was arrested. People decided to take action.

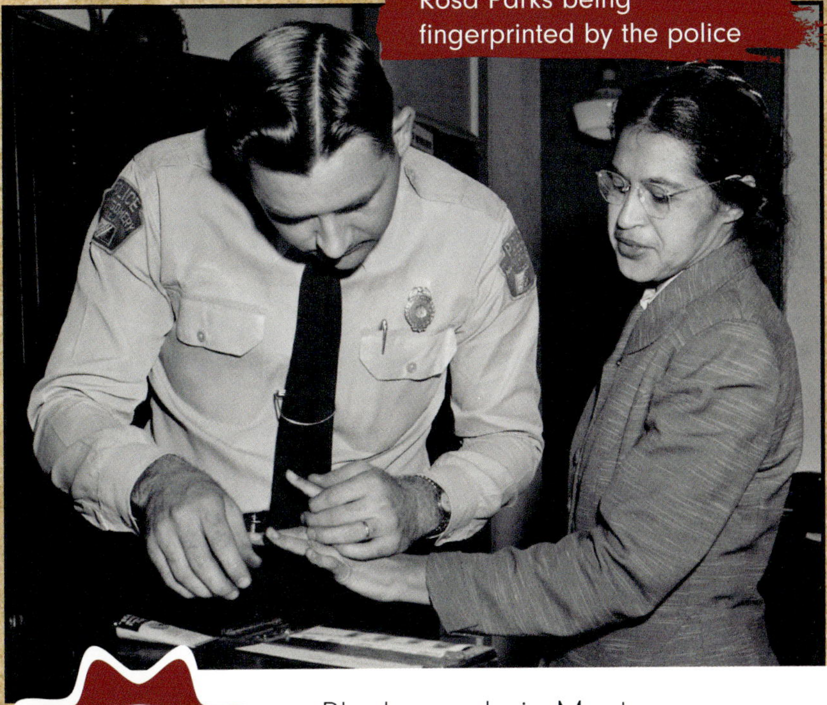

Rosa Parks being fingerprinted by the police

Learn More

Black people in Montgomery were made to sit in the back of the bus. If the front was full, they were supposed to give their seats to white people.

Rosa Parks

Civil rights leaders started the Montgomery Bus **Boycott**. It aimed to desegregate, or stop the separation of races, on buses. One leader of the boycott was Dr. Martin Luther King Jr. For more than a year, Black people in Montgomery refused to take city buses.

Learn More

Bus segregation was ruled unconstitutional by the Supreme Court in 1956.

Protesting Segregation

People fought segregation in other places too. One of the ways they did this was called a sit-in. During this peaceful protest, people sat in segregated places such as restaurants and businesses until they were served.

sit-in, 1960,
Durham, North Carolina

Learn More

A protest is an event at which a group objects to an idea, an act, or a way of doing something.

sit-in, 1960,
Atlanta, Georgia

By 1960, Supreme Court cases had desegregated other places, including bus stations. To fight segregation that was still taking place, **supporters** of the civil rights movement began Freedom Rides. They rode buses through the South and used facilities they weren't supposed to.

Learn More

Freedom Riders often weren't welcomed. They were beaten and arrested at times. One bus was set on fire.

POLICE DEPT. JACKSON, MISS 21095 7-2-61
POLICE DEPT. JACKSON, MISS 21049
POLICE DEPT. JACKSON, MISS 21043
POLICE DEPT. JACKSON, MISS 21016
POLICE DEPT. JACKSON, MISS 21042
POLICE DEPT. JACKSON, MISS 21098 7-2-61
POLICE DEPT. JACKSON, MISS 21031
POLICE DEPT. JACKSON, MISS 21032
POLICE DEPT. JACKSON, MISS 21034
POLICE DEPT. JACKSON, MISS 21036
POLICE DEPT. JACKSON, MISS
POLICE DEPT. JACKSON, MISS 21035
POLICE DEPT. JACKSON, MISS 21030
POLICE DEPT. JACKSON, MISS 21033
POLICE DEPT. JACKSON, MISS 21038

YTH & SON GRO.
ELL·O
K·ICE CREAM

Marching on Washington

The March on Washington for Jobs and Freedom took place on August 28, 1963. It was a big moment in the civil rights movement. More than 200,000 people gathered in Washington, DC, to show support for Black Americans' civil rights.

Learn More

Dr. Martin Luther King Jr. gave his powerful "I Have a Dream" speech at the march. Many people were moved by his words and asked for new equality laws.

Laws for Equality

Congress passed the Civil Rights Act of 1964 to fight discrimination based on race, color, **religion**, or the country someone came from. It also banned segregation in public places. The Voting Rights Act of 1965 banned practices that stopped Black Americans from voting.

Learn More

Dr. Martin Luther King Jr. was present when President Lyndon Johnson signed the Civil Rights Act of 1964.

Malcolm X

Many leaders of the civil rights movement believed in Martin Luther King Jr.'s use of peaceful protest. Malcolm X did not at first. He thought more forceful methods might be needed. He spoke powerfully of Black pride and had many followers.

Learn More

Malcolm X later came to believe that all people could live peacefully together. He was killed on February 21, 1965.

King Is Killed

On April 5, 1968, Martin Luther King Jr. was killed in Memphis, Tennessee. This didn't end the civil rights movement, but supporters were never as **united** again. Some joined **militant** groups such as the Black Panther Party. Others tried to make changes by working in the U.S. government.

Learn More

Today, Americans continue to fight discrimination through groups and protests.

Timeline of the Civil Rights Movement

1954
The Supreme Court rules "separate but equal" is unconstitutional in *Brown v. Board of Education of Topeka.*

1955
Rosa Parks is arrested in Montgomery, Alabama, for not giving up her bus seat. A bus boycott begins.

1961
The first Freedom Rides take place.

1963
The March on Washington takes place. Dr. Martin Luther King Jr. gives his "I Have a Dream" speech.

1964
The Civil Rights Act is passed.

1965
Malcolm X is killed. The Voting Rights Act is passed.

1968
Martin Luther King Jr. is killed.

Glossary

amendment: A change or addition to a constitution.

boycott: The act of refusing to have dealings with a person or business to force change.

cemetery: A place where the dead are buried.

citizen: Someone who lives in a country legally and has certain rights.

enslaved: Having to do with being owned by another person and forced to work without pay.

facility: Something built for a purpose.

integrated: Desegregated, or combined.

militant: Describing a group who will use force to support a cause or beliefs.

offensive: Causing hurt, anger, or upset.

race: A group that people are often divided into based on physical features thought to be common among those with a shared heritage.

religion: The beliefs and ways of honoring a god or gods.

supporter: Someone who supports, or holds up and helps.

united: Working together to achieve a goal.

For More Information

Books

King, Martin Luther, Jr. *I Have a Dream*. New York, NY: Ann Schwartz Books, 2025.

London, Martha. *Civil Rights*. Minneapolis, MN: Bearport Publishing, 2023.

Website

The Civil Rights Trail
civilrightstrail.com
Find out if one of these civil rights landmarks is near you and learn more about them all.

Publisher's note to educators and parents: *Our editors have carefully reviewed these websites to ensure that they are suitable for students. Many websites change frequently, however, and we cannot guarantee that a site's future contents will continue to meet our high standards of quality and educational value. Be advised that students should be closely supervised whenever they access the internet.*

Index

American Civil War, 4
Black Panther Party, 28
boycotts, 16, 30
Civil Rights Act, 24, 25, 30
Freedom Rides, 20, 30
Johnson, Lyndon, 25
King, Martin Luther, Jr., 16, 22, 25, 26, 28, 30
Malcolm X, 26, 27, 30
Memphis, Tennessee, 28
Montgomery, Alabama, 14, 15, 16, 30
NAACP, 12
Parks, Rosa, 14, 30
sit-ins, 18
U.S. Supreme Court, 8, 12, 17, 20, 30
Voting Rights Act, 24, 30